Restorative Practices

Better Outcomes Through
Solution Fluency

Lee Watanabe-Crockett

WABISABI Ⓦ LEARNING
www.wabisabilearning.com

WABISABI Ⓦ LEARNING

ISBN: 9781098652234

Published by:

Wabisabi Learning
#201-4501 Kingsway
Burnaby BC, V5H 0E5

https://www.wabisabilearning.com

For more information about this book or the authors, please contact us at hello@wabisabizen.com or visit our website at www.wabisabilearning.com

Contents

Section 3: Using Solution Fluency for Restorative Practice

Section 4: Managing Restorative Practice

About the Author

Lee Watanabe-Crockett is an author, keynote speaker, inspirational thinker, and an optimist who believes in a bright future and our ability to build it together through connection and compassion. He works with governments, education systems, international agencies, and corporations to help people and organisations connect to their highest purpose and realise their wishes for the future.

Lee believes in creating balance in the reality of a digital present and future. As such, living in Japan, he studies Aikido, Buddhism, and the Shakuhachi, a traditional Japanese bamboo flute. Joyful curiosity is the foundation of his approach to creating vital learning environments for groups around the world.

Several of his best-selling books including *Literacy is Not Enough*, *Growing Global Digital Citizens*, *Mindful Assessment*, and his most recent *Future-Focused Learning: 10 Essential Shifts of Everyday Practice* have garnered many awards and are used in schools and universities around the world.

Introducing
Solution Fluency and
Restorative Practice

What is Restorative Practice?

Restorative practice is a system of proactive conflict resolution and management that includes addressing the needs of the victim, the offender, and the affected community. It seeks to promote healthy relationships and encourage association, and to lay the foundation for developing the interpersonal skills and emotional awareness that can turn human conflict into an opportunity for growth and healing.

Whereas punitive practices focus primarily on exclusion, blame, criminalization, and decisive punishment for the wrongdoer (and hopefully justice for the victim), restorative practices are based on inclusion, compassion, and fostering proactive connection and communication. Restorative practice seeks to avoid blame and guilt, and eschew the "eye for an eye" mentality that victims often feel, striving instead for an open dialogue that seeks to nurture understanding and awareness between all involved parties. It removes the need for revenge and engages all participants in finding a solution that lasts. However, it does not negate consequence.

It was Howard Zehr's 1990 book *Changing Lenses: A New Focus for Crime and Justice* that brought widespread awareness to restorative practices. As a result, the assumption is that it is a more recent development. However, restorative approaches have appeared in many cultures throughout history including Roman, Babylonian, African, Asian, Celtic, Native American, and countless others.

Why Use Restorative Practice In Schools?

According to "School-Wide Restorative Practices: Step by Step," a white paper published in 2017 by the Denver School-Based Restorative Practices Partnership, punitive practices began to increase in schools dramatically in the 1980s. This was part of a zero-tolerance stand taken on disruptive youth behaviour. It meant that suspensions, expulsions, and law enforcement referrals increased even for the most minor of offences. The problem is that these punitive practices hardly ever result in any improvement in student behaviour.

Instead, punitive approaches alienate students from their classrooms and from their peers, and exclude them from receiving a quality education—sometimes unjustly.

This succeeds in accomplishing little more than a renewed contempt for the school system and community due to the negative connotations associated with it through punitive practices. Restorative practices, however, are about enhancing the school community by embracing the humanity in both victim and offender. It's about solving problems rather than meting out punishment. But how does this benefit schools?

Simply put, healthier and happier schools produce healthier and happier citizens. Forward-thinking and inclusive, restorative practice provides a pathway to building trust among students and staff, thereby increasing engagement and the passion for learning in a comfortable and supportive environment.

Introducing Solution Fluency

As much as restorative practices are aimed at addressing matters concerning good communication and relationships, they are also fundamentally a system for solving problems and modelling ethical behaviour and respect for all. The reason this is so significant is because in our travels we have asked practically every educator we meet what they believe are the most important skills for our children to learn for leading successful lives beyond school. Overwhelmingly, the consensus is that students need transparency-level skills in these areas:

- Problem solving
- Creativity
- Analytic thinking
- Collaboration
- Communication
- Ethics, action, and accountability

As it turns out, cultivating problem-solving skills is a top priority, a sentiment which is echoed in curricula around the world including New Zealand's key competencies, the International Baccalaureate's IB Learner Profile, the Common Core Standards Initiative, and many more. In other words, educators around the world agree that learning how to independently solve problems is one of the most vital academic pursuits our modern learners can undertake during the time they spend in school. Problem-solving skills are more than just skills for learning—they're skills for life.

It was important to us in our mission of serving both learners and their teachers to produce an unconscious intutive process that would allow anyone to solve any problem regardless of its scope or severity. We wanted to be able to show learners "what to do when you don't know what to do." And so, Solution Fluency was born.

We introduced Solution Fluency in our bestselling book *Mindful Assessment* (2017) as a universal structured problem-solving process, as well as an essential system for building great problem-solving prowess and critical thinking capacity. The children of today who will be the leaders of tomorrow will need a process they can internalize for facing challenges and solving problems that really matter. We've come to know this process as the 6 Ds of Solution Fluency. The following descriptions have been adapted from the *Mindful Assessment* book (Crockett & Churches, 2017).

1. Define

First, we clearly define what the problem is in order to solve it. In doing so we provide context and a list of potential solutions. However, we must also be able to reflect critically and independently on the purpose and sequence, asking ourselves "What do I need to do?" This requires breaking tasks down to component elements, sequencing them logically, understanding how to apply tasks and skills to the process, and evaluating completeness.

2. Discover

If the define question asks "What do I need to do?" the discover question asks "What do I need to know and be able to do?" This stage is about exploring the background of the problem and gathering information about its nature and severity. In order to do this effectively, a series of probing and inquiring questions must be asked to help us find the information we seek. In addition, discovering also means accessing a range of suitable and authoritative primary and secondary information sources, and then evaluating each information source's validity.

3. Dream

In the dream stage, learners open their hearts and minds to possibilities and visions of a solution they way they want to see it. This phase is about imagination, extrapolation, and visualization. One of the greatest challenges in dream is to truly embrace the possibilities. This is because it's far more common for us to focus on all the

reasons why something can't be done. In our experience, primary school students are much less resistant to this process than adults. Young minds are not fettered with the shackles of limiting beliefs such as "I'm not smart enough" or "it's too big a problem for us to solve" or "it's never been done before, so why now?" This is why it is so critical to develop problem-solving skills at an early age.

4. Design

This stage sees us using our gathered knowledge to actually synthesize solutions. This means we create goals and milestones, assign team roles, and create accountability systems for the whole team. Starting with a future point in mind and working backward is how this process is built. With a firm vision of the successful future outcome, we begin by asking "Where do we want to be?" followed by designing a response to the question "How are we going to get there?"

5. Deliver

Designing a presentation isn't enough; it has to be presented. Writing a song isn't enough; it has to be performed. Developing a script isn't enough; it has to be rehearsed and staged. In other words, at some point we've got to deliver the goods. It is impossible to determine if you've solved the original problem if you don't know whether your solution will even work or not, so the only way to find out is by putting it into action. We ask ourselves "How do I make it happen?" or "How am I going to get there?" This phase happens in two separate stages—(1) produce and (2) publish. It involves both completing the solution (produce) and then making the actual presentation or demonstration (publish).

6. Debrief

During a debrief, students look at their projects from beginning to end and really get to own their learning. They determine what they could have done better and how they could improve their problem-solving approach in similar situations. The problem becomes personal when we take ownership of it, which helps us develop a sense of accountability. This is where we consider the questions "What were my results, and what did I learn from them? How could I make this product and the process better?" In our experience, once students have been involved in the debrief phase, they start to prepare by themselves and make improvements to their products before they present them.

How Solution Fluency is Being Used in Restorative Practice

When we introduced Solution Fluency, we knew it was an essential skill. We had visualized a comprehensive approach that could be easily taught to students, and a cyclical all-encompassing process that could be used in any application. However, we didn't foresee many of the things that did come to pass, including just how versatile a process it would become and how far-reaching its applications could be. This came to us when we learned that many of the schools we work with were having success using Solution Fluency for conflict resolution. If you think about it, this makes perfect sense. Solution Fluency is, after all, a structured process for solving virtually any problem imaginable no matter how big or small. Why wouldn't it work for conflict resolution and restorative practices?

The first occurrence of students using Solution Fluency for conflict resolution was at St. Timothy School in Edmonton, Alberta. According to principal Phebe Switzer, two students had come to her asking to use Solution Fluency to solve their quarrel instead of receiving outside judgment. An excellent administrator and a very quick thinker, Ms. Switzer took the opportunity to facilitate the process for them gladly.

Each began by Defining the problem from their perspective. Next, the students used Discover to determine where the issue had come from and were able to understand each other's perspective. They then collaborated on a Dream—a solution to the problem that would satisfy both their concerns. Once agreed upon, they built a simple plan or Design for implementation and then Delivered that plan. They met back with the principal at a prearranged time to Debrief the process and to ensure the problem had been solved. Since this instance, students at St. Timothy regularly engage in the same process on their own, outside the influence and control of administrators, with much success.

A nearly identical scenario occurred not long after at St. Jerome, another primary school in the Edmonton Catholic School District. Apparently, this was no coincidence, so we began speaking to other schools we had worked with that were using Solution Fluency. Our inquiries revealed that this was an organic development in many schools and an unexpected benefit of engaging students in the Solution Fluency process. In addition to this, an excellent school in Tasmania, Youngstown Primary, when hearing of encounters

in other schools, took proactive action. Alongside the school-wide rollout of inquiry using Solution Fluency, they developed a strategy for restorative applications to help reinforce the 6 Ds to students as a process not just for problems presented in the classroom.

A now-familiar pattern has also emerged in several primary schools around the globe. As learners are empowered with Solution Fluency and begin to recognize their capacity to solve problems, they seek to apply it outside the classroom. At some point, two students will end up in conflict and find themselves before their principal, and one of them recommends that they use Solution Fluency to solve the problem. It seems natural to them to apply a problem-solving process they have used in class to other issues, and this transfer of skills is what we strive for as educators.

Summary

In this section we've discussed what restorative practices are and how they compare to traditional punitive measures in regard to core intentions and outcomes. We've also explored why schools should consider adopting them in lieu of punitive practices, and introduced a few schools that have incorporated RP successfully. In addition, we've provided a review of what Solution Fluency is and the process that defines it.

In the sections that follow, we'll discuss how to get started with restorative practices as well as how the 6 Ds of Solution Fluency provide the perfect framework for maximizing the benefits of restorative practices in your school.

Guiding Questions

- What are "restorative practices?"
- How do they differ from traditional punitive measures?
- How can schools benefit from incorporating restorative practices in place of traditional punitive practice?
- What are the 6 Ds of Solution Fluency and why are they the ideal framework for implementing restorative practices?

Beginning
Restorative Practice

RP Core Philosophies

Since restorative practices are life skills, they are built around certain core beliefs and ideas that make them unique in the world of conflict resolution. We'll begin this section by discussing what some of those ideas are and how they inform the practice of RP.

In the traditional punitive system of student discipline we ask:

- What rule was broken?
- Who did it?
- What is the punishment?

Restorative practice asks:

- What happened?
- Who has been affected?
- What are we going to do to make things right?

Incidents that arise from conflict have what's called a "ripple effect." As you can see from the graphic on the right, the initial event has an immediate impact on both the instigator and the victim. From there, the damage can potentially extend to family members on both sides as well as the general community, depending on factors like the scope and severity of the incident. This ripple effect is the main reason why restorative practices take into account the viewpoints of individuals and groups that extend beyond those of the victim(s) and the perpetrator(s).

The Laws of Conflict

Conflict is the very reason for the existence of restorative practices. Conflict between people and groups is a fact of life, and RP is the most ideal method for addressing it, especially in educational settings. Let's take a closer look at the nature of conflict.

1. Conflict is Both Natural and Inevitable

Humans are unique, complex and multidimensional, and our personalities vary significantly from individual to individual. Also, we tend to attach importance to

different wants and needs between youth and adulthood, and when we feel these needs are not being acknowledged or met, conflict with others will inevitably arise. This is a crucial thing to remember when it comes to our students.

At one time or another, to one degree or another, we will experience friction with someone else. To assimilate this into our lives in a healthy way, it pays to internalize a proactive social-emotional skill set for managing personal conflicts.

2. There Are Different Forms of Conflict

Types of conflict can be broken down into 4 primary groups:

- Intrapersonal (conflict within ourselves)
- Interpersonal (conflict with another person)
- Intragroup (conflict within a group)
- Intergroup (conflict between one or more groups)

Generally, conflict occurs as a result of two people or groups wanting different outcomes in a particular situation or interaction. As for what fuels it, the fact is that people and groups can spiral into conflict over practically anything, from the most mundane to the most paramount of issues. It depends on who is involved and how badly they desire their own outcome.

3. Conflict Can Be Both Good and Bad

This is usually determined by how we deal with it, but the conflict has the potential to be either highly damaging or very productive. Factors that determine this generally come down to the personalities of those involved, their level of experience with conflict management, their social-emotional skills, and the personal values they hold most dear, among other things.

Managing Expectations: Myths and Facts

Chances are you've heard conflicting things about restorative practices. Many of the organizations using it, educational or otherwise, swear by it. Others put less faith in its ability to right wrongs and bring balance to a conflict situation. Let's address some common misunderstandings about RP and attempt to set the record straight.

What RP Is and Is Not

MYTH: *RP is just people sitting in circles talking about their feelings.*

FACT: RP involves using the problem-solving processes of conflict management, embodied in this case by the 6Ds of Solution Fluency. Yes, feelings are brought to bear, but so are personal histories, motivations, regrets, and most importantly collaborative

ideas for holistic long-term solutions to conflict. It can also be done in circles, but this is only one way to do it.

MYTH: *We're already doing it.*

FACT: You may be to some degree, but chances are its effectiveness is not being measured or maintained in any structured way. In fact, more often than not it is a personal choice made by teachers or students who believe in it but may not have sufficient experience with it. Correct RP requires a deep commitment from both staff and students to specific practices for attaining measurable results over an extended period of time.

MYTH: *RP is soft and doesn't bring justice to the victim.*

FACT: RP is about a different kind of result, namely understanding. The purpose of RP is to repair as much emotional and psychological damage as possible and to avoid further harm, not seek punitive compensation for wrongdoing. Not being rooted in such measures, it's true that it isn't the kind of "swift justice" that we think happens when decisive punishment is administered. More often than not, however, the adverse effects of traditional punitive measures far outweigh their benefits. RP seeks to make all voices heard and to attain a mode of justice for the victim through a reconciliation with the wrongdoer, and the cooperative rehabilitation of everyone involved. In this way, all are healed and restored.

MYTH: *RP takes away from a teacher's authority.*

FACT: Many teachers resist restorative practices because they feel it gives them less choice on how to deal with those who may be creating a disruptive or unsafe environment in their classrooms. RP works to actually give teachers more transformative tools for bringing order to learning environments.

MYTH: *RP takes too long.*

FACT: It takes no more time to implement in a school system than punitive practices, but with beneficial differences. Punitive methods mostly fail to address and correct the underlying motivations behind a conflict. As a result, there is no shared understanding

and conflict continues'. However, RP takes an in-depth look at the causes of the conflict and focuses on relationship building and repairing. In the beginning, RP will take a time investment, and the results aren't immediate. That said, it saves time in the long run since underlying issues are addressed and fixed by the application of a set of practices that can be used again and again in different situations. As relationships strengthen through practice, conflicts become less frequent and are addressed more effectively using these practices, before they have a chance to spiral out of control.

MYTH: *RP won't work with our staff and students.*

FACT: This is like assuming students all learn the same way, which we know as educators to be entirely untrue. Restorative practices are, by nature, resilient and adaptable. This is the precise reason why organizations tend to adopt them in their own way and at their own pace. It's not to say that a system used to traditional approaches won't have a challenge ahead of them in adjusting. What must be understood is that, like anything new, a solid plan is required.

Embracing Realities: What to Expect

When adopting any new framework of discipline, there will always be preconceived notions of how things should progress. It's no different when bringing restorative practice into a school that has never adopted such methods before. However, administrators and staff must be willing to curb expectations and exhibit patience while the new practices gain a foothold in school culture.

With that said, here are some of the truths about introducing the benefits of restorative practices in your school.

It's going to take at least some time.

The current discipline practices being used in schools largely echo the criminal justice system, and it's been this way for many years. Restorative practices are very divergent from these punitive measures and are a radically different approach to conflict management. Adopting these practices means taking on new training, new procedures, and new mindsets. This all takes time to embed itself in the school and community consciousness.

Don't look for the quick fix when considering RP. You'll need to be patient with yourself and with others, and you'll need to work hard to make it successful. The results will be more than worth the effort.

You will have to determine your readiness and then plan accordingly. Before you, your school, or your district begin this venture, you need two things. First, you need to know where you are now; secondly, you need to know where you want to be. This is where you start with the end in mind. A pre-implementation audit can help you achieve a snapshot.

It will involve ongoing training, development, and check-ins.

RP is a professional practice that requires a consistent schedule of training and professional development for practitioners. In addition to this, a series of scheduled monthly check-in meetings for keeping the lines of communication open and reporting on progress is a good practice.

The first year will be the most important, and the most difficult.

So much will be revealed to you in your first year with RP, and it will indicate how you should best move forward for the higher good of your school and your community. Remember that this is an entire cultural shift happening, and it can seem overwhelming. Be patient and keep focused on what the data is telling you. As you progress with RP, data analysis will be an ongoing procedure for ensuring your program is functioning optimally.

Analyzing your first year of data will help you determine how staff and students are adjusting to these new practices and internalizing the philosophy of RP. It will show you improvement in areas you may not have expected, and it will also fall short of your expectations in some areas. The most important thing is that it will show where you need to improve and revise ideas.

The Limits of Restorative Practice

One particular story of restorative practice to consider is a 1993 New Zealand news story referenced by Jim Consedine in his book *Restorative Justice: Healing the Effects of Crime* (1995). It concerns a 20-year-old Samoan man who killed 2 boys

from South Auckland with his car. According to the story, the boy's families met with him for a grief-sharing and reconciliation celebration that included both Tongan and Samoan attendees at a ceremony at the Methodist Church, followed by a full reconciliation and his being welcomed back into both communities.

Although this is an incredible story representing what restorative practice can achieve, the truth is it's the exception and not the rule. In fact, most restorative practice outcomes will be relatively modest and even a bit shaky. No conflict management philosophy or system is perfect. Any school interested in embracing restorative practices must be aware of the realities regarding its limitations.

Think of it this way: after restorative conversations have been introduced after a school incident, the result may be that you have two people—often two young and impressionable people—who have been asked to step outside their emotional comfort zones. As a result, they're a bit emotionally raw, and perhaps not entirely sure what's just happened or what's expected of them. Chances are it won't be how they imagined the situation would have been handled.

People can be fiercely protective of how they feel, and many of us would more often rather be "right" than be "kind"—it's merely human nature. Restorative practice as a system of addressing conflict takes time to get used to, and also to see results from. However, that's a small price to pay considering we are still waiting to see positive results in schools from punitive measures that have been in place for several decades.

Consider also students with limited cognitive ability, low moral maturity, reduced empathy, or just difficulty seeing things from another's perspective. How can they be expected to respond to restorative approaches in conflicts they're involved in? This can create a significant power imbalance between such participants and the RP mediator, mainly when the victim's distress is very high. These limits do not detract from RP as they also apply to other justice models. Nevertheless, educators need to be aware of these possibilities coming into play, so they don't end up doing more harm than good.

What You Need to Get Going

Some basic things need to be in place for beginning with restorative practices. Let's take a brief look below at what are likely some of the most important ones to consider.

Purpose

Understanding your purpose for adopting restorative practices begins with knowing where you are currently. It's imperative that meaningful conversations happen around RP before anything is planned or implemented, and one of the primary reflections you will all have to make as an administrative team is "Why are we doing this?"

As explorations commence, you'll need to be prepared for total honesty and transparency. The questions you ask will likely give rise to other matters, and the more you uncover in a constructive and collaborative atmosphere, the clearer and more achievable your goals will be.

Discussion questions for the administrative team can include, but are not limited to, the following:

- How would we describe the current conflict resolution and discipline practices in our school?
- How would we describe their success over _____ number of years?
- What is it about them that isn't working to make us consider RP?
- What does the research tell us about the effectiveness of RP in other schools?
- Who can we talk to that has had success with RP?
- What do we ultimately want to achieve with RP?
- How do we want our students/staff/community to benefit from RP?

The following factors should be considered and discussed when deciding if your school is ready to enter a restorative practices program:

- What are the current needs of the school community in relation to restorative practices?
- How do you feel restorative practices could address these needs?
- Have restorative practices been considered by your school before? If so, what prevented you from implementing them previously?
- Does your school have facilities/environments/spaces that are suitable for restorative practices to be effectively utilized?
- Is there a solid commitment from staff and administration to restorative practices?

- Are staff and administration prepared to attend any necessary introductory training and orientation?
- Would you be hiring an official RP coordinator as a new staff member, or is training someone internally to take on the role more preferable?
- Does the leadership of the school have a collaborative style?
- What does the school community already know about restorative practices?
- What do you think are the primary strengths/weaknesses of restorative practices?
- What resistance to restorative practices may exist in the school?
- When would be the best time to introduce restorative practices to the school?
- Are there any current school programs or initiatives you feel would be compatible with restorative practices? If so, what are they?

School Climate

Another crucial consideration is if your school is adequately climatized to facilitate a switch to RP as an effective conflict management solution. Ask questions like:

- Does our school offer a safe, fair, and positive learning environment?
- Is the need for punitive disciplinary practices higher than it should be?
- Do staff or community stakeholders have any concerns about the harmful effects of traditional punitive methods?
- Do we have the necessary physical space, and if not, can we produce it?

Head RP Coordinator

This is the central figure who will act as guide and administrator of RP practices in your school. Depending on your situation, you may choose to either hire someone to fill this role or train someone from your school/district internally. The Center for Restorative Programs lists these as the top qualities preferred in an RP coordinator:

- Training in group facilitation, conflict resolution, and restorative justice approaches
- Experience with youth empowerment models and/or restorative justice/discipline in schools
- Experience with trauma-informed care and family-focused approaches

- Strong organizational, communication and written skills
- Ability to develop community contacts and initiate program delivery in an independent fashion
- Ability to understand and be open to different cultures and communities
- Ability to work effectively with individuals of different ages and backgrounds
- Ability to work within a team structure and with related program policies/procedures
- Ability to prioritize, respond and adapt to variable program priorities and cycles
- Ability to collaborate with school personnel and families
- Strong commitment to helping build community and repair relationships

Your RP coordinator will also train others to act as additional guides or assistants in your RP practices, depending on your number of students and your level of need.

Buy-In

As we have discussed, the success of restorative practices calls on the acceptance and support of both your school staff and the members of the wider community. This primarily means the parents of the children you teach.

Look forward to enlightening and challenging conversations with students, staff, and parents about the future of RP in your school. Like it or not, you're going to encounter resistance to the idea from individuals who either don't fully understand it or are just too mired in old mindsets to give it a chance. Nevertheless, it's up to you and your team to decide how and why RP is a step in the right direction for the welfare of your school, district, and community, and to convince others to follow your lead.

For the preliminary talks, make as solid a case as possible for RP implementation and welcome every bit of the input you'll receive. Ensure everyone you talk to knows that in the restorative spirit, all opinions and concerns are heard and no voices go ignored.

Summary

This section has taken you on a deeper dive into the philosophies, core beliefs, and realities of restorative practices. You've recieved some guidance on what kinds of questions to ask when choosing to explore these practices in your school, and what you can expect to have happen in your journey. With these tools to assist you, it's now time to take a look at how a restorative practice session might look as implemented using the 6 Ds framework of Solution Fluency.

Guiding Questions

- What are the core philosophies of restorative practices?
- Why do people experience conflict, and how can restorative practices help?
- Who is affected by the "Ripple Effect" in a conflict situation, and how are they affected?
- What are some of the realities of implementing restorative practices, and why are they vital for schools to consider?
- What does your school need to have in place before restorative practices can be successfully adopted?

Using Solution Fluency for
Restorative Practice

Aligning 6 D and RP

In the following sections we'll explore a step-by-step roadmap for using Solution Fluency in restorative conversations. Each phase of the 6Ds begins with a brief explanation and is supported by exploratory questions asked at each step, and these coincide with the questions we also ask during the stages of restorative practices.

What follows serves as a set of guidelines for you to consider for using Solution Fluency in restorative practices. It is intended as a framework from which we encourage you to develop your own process.

Warm Up by Cooling Down—Practical Beginnings

Let's assume that there has been an incident in the school between a pair of students that warrants using restorative practices. Do you straight away snatch up the students and witnesses, haul them into a room, sit them in a circle and hope that RP does its thing? Absolutely not—that's the shortest road to ensuring restorative conversations end up doing more harm than good.

To get the right perspective, think about what is going on right after an altercation. Tempers are high, feelings are mixed, tensions are palpable, and everyone involved is predictably upset. Diving right into a restorative conversation is entirely the wrong thing to do here. Remember that RP is a delicate process for repairing relationships and making meaningful connections, not a magic pill for every disagreement students and staff get into. As such, it has to be implemented tactfully.

Initially, after an incident that will need RP, it's recommended that a brief "cool-down" period be allowed to take place. This gives everyone involved a chance to calm down, process the events, and reflect on what has happened. How much time this period takes may well depend on different factors including the number of people involved, who they were, and the severity of the incident. You can end up conducting RP up to days after an event. It all depends on those involved and their needs and abilities, which are the crucial consideration.

Keep an eye on the involved parties during this period and respond to their needs as appropriate. You'll find some individuals will have a more difficult time coping than others, which will inform how you manage cool-down periods before even beginning to

use a restorative conversation. On the other hand, a more minor situation can resolve itself on its own during this cool-down period, thereby eliminating the need for a restorative discussion altogether.

Agreement or Consent

In the beginning, there needs to be an agreement for all parties to work through RP. There has to be some acknowledgment of there being a problem because ultimately restorative practices are concerned with fixing that problem, not laying the blame. In most cases, parental consent forms may need to be distributed or signed agreements shared between all parties to ensure everyone is on board with the process. Make sure everyone knows why they are being called together and work to determine what the best shared goals are. This is something that participants must be made fully aware of at the beginning of any RP session. It will set the tone for progress and ensure everyone knows they are part of an effective practice that will see everyone cared for and all voices heard.

The 6 D Process in Restorative Practice

1. Define

To solve a problem, we have to clearly define it is first. We must decide what needs to be addressed and give proper context to the problem.

SF Questions: What are the details of our challenge? What do we want to overcome specifically? What do we want to solve?

RP Questions: What happened? Who was involved? Where did the incident take place? What were the events leading to the conflict?

In this initial stage, we are trying to get a clear picture of the problem that has called together the RP meeting. Discover what the problem is from each person's point of view, both victim and offender. What actually happened in the incident in question? What did the teacher involved observe?

It is important to note also that, in many cases, the teacher may not always have been present. That means other students who have witnessed the event may need to be involved in the process and be asked these questions. This is the optimal time to model the respect and attentiveness we want our learners to develop as they are exposed to restorative practices.

- Listen actively and pay close attention to how the person speaking is using their language.
- Let each person have their full say, no matter what it may be. In other words, if they use this opportunity to justify their actions, allow them to do so.
- Make sure only one person speaks at a time, and state that everyone will have a chance to be heard.
- Remind participants that total honesty is absolutely critical. They must know that this is a safe place to speak openly and without judgment.
- Cultivate and encourage an atmosphere of respect for everyone.
- Ask questions and check for understanding. This applies to every stage where mediation and facilitation are involved. Remember, don't tell when you can ask instead.
- Students are often acquiescent—seek authentic understanding rather than just an agreement to get through the process quickly. This is a risk in the time-limited world of education.
- Have a process in place for documentation of incidents, i.e., incident reports. Most schools will have procedures that include each party (and a teacher, if they witnessed the incident) writing their own reports.

2. Discover

This is stage for primarily researching and analyzing knowledge about the problem so that we can identify with it more easily.

SF Questions: What do we need to know? Why do we need this to happen? What can we change?

RP Questions: What is everyone's specific account of the incident? What was each person thinking and feeling? What is the history between the people involved, if any? What has happened since the incident took place?

Now to get the history of what has gone on between the two involved parties. Get each person's perspective of what has happened to bring them to where they are now. How were they feeling and what were they thinking at the time the incident happened? What were the specific needs each of them had that they felt weren't being fulfilled?

It's also important at this stage to discuss what has happened since then and who else may have been affected by the incident. This is where the outlook of parents and the community come into consideration.

- In this stage, uncomfortable feelings and emotions may surface. Again, remind participants they are in a safe and judgment-free zone.

- Each person in a dispute interprets the other's intentions through a filter of their own individual anger, pain, and fear. Encourage participants to limit assumptions about another's motivations and merely focus on how they are feeling personally.

- Respond to each participant with empathetic, non-threatening body language and facial expressions.

- Many smaller incidents, if left unaddressed, can often lead to larger conflicts down the road. Try to determine what unresolved past events may have had an impact on what has happened.

- If someone wants to apologize, let it happen. Participants must feel they are there to be heard and not corrected.

3. Dream

Here, we open up the heart and mind to envisioning a solution the way we wish to see it. This phase is all about imagination and extrapolation.

SF Questions: What do we truly want to create? How will it function? What will it look like? What's our best-case scenario for the end goal we want to achieve?

RP Questions: What have you thought about since then? What do you want to have happen? Why do you feel this is the best outcome for everyone?

Here the RP coordinator now strives to bring awareness to those involved of what they feel would be the most ideal solution to the conflict. What would be the best outcome that would benefit all parties involved in the dispute?

- Often you'll hear a response like "being friends." Make it clear that not everyone has to become friends, but everyone does need to respect each other.

- This is a perfect time to allow students to collaborate on a solution to the problem that would satisfy both their concerns if they wish to do so.

- Ensuring participants have a chance to demonstrate a willingness to change their behaviour is far more effective than administering punishment as it is a chance for them to learn from mistakes.

 # 4. Design

This is the workshopping phase where the mechanics of your solution take shape, allowing us to get the solution "on paper."

SF Questions: How will we create our solution? What are the steps we'll take? What are the milestones and guidelines we will set for ourselves? How will we deal with problems?

RP Questions: What do you think you need to do to make things right? What are the steps we need to take? How can we work together to facilitate them?

It's time now for both parties to work together to design the most beneficial and harmonious solution for moving forward and repairing any harm that was done. This must be carefully facilitated in the appropriate direction by the RP coordinator as it has a direct impact on the next phase.

Remember also that Solution Fluency is a cyclical process. As such, it is not uncommon to have to revisit previous stages of the process if new problems arise or there are still questions unanswered. What's important is designing a restorative solution that works for everyone. It may take extra time, and that's perfectly normal and acceptable.

Here are some suggestions for things to consider in this stage:

- Determining what individual and group responsibilities will be

- Projecting the desired outcome and constructing a timeline for action, including when a follow-up meeting will be held to check on participants' progress

- Setting up a system of accountability to themselves and each other

- Creating opportunities for formaland informal check-ins

5. Deliver

This phase has two stages—Produce and Publish. It includes both completing the product (Produce) and presenting the proposed solution (Publish).

SF Questions: How do we bring this idea into reality? How do we practically apply what we've done? How will we know it's working?

RP Questions: How do we proceed with our solution? How do we keep track of progress? What are the procedures for dealing with any challenges along the way?

With Solution Fluency, it is essential that any plan is put into action actually to test the viability of the solution. In restorative practices, the same thing needs to happen. Beyond the dreaming and the discussions, participants must do the hard work that is necessary for repairing damaged relationships. Actually working on making things right is always better than punishment.

Neuroscience tells us that each brain is unique and in a constant state of growth and change. It's important to remember that a child's mind is a work in progress. It's dangerous to assume that all students come to school with an ability to decode value systems. Facilitators will need to be there as guides and support networks if required.

- Each participant is expected to take responsibility for their actions in whatever way was decided on in the Dream and Design phases.
- This stage may involve students having reconciliatory discussions with affected parents and members of the community. Such discussions should be carefully mediated by the RP coordinator or an assistant where possible.
- Parents and community members who are also profoundly affected by the incident may have ongoing questions and concerns that must be addressed.
- Parents should be contacted at the end of any RP process so they're aware of the outcomes and process, and learning can be discussed in the home environment.
- Students will have behaviours that may need changing, which can take time to become habits. Making the process as constructive and safe as possible will help this, and guide them towards strategies that may assist them in the future.
- Apologies which need to be made can happen at this stage if they haven't previously. There's never a wrong or inappropriate time for this to take place.

Another suggestion for this stage is to implement a series of check-ins for updating progress between the main parties involved. As with any other instance in which Solution Fluency is used, previous stages may need to be revisitied if problems arise during the period of reconciliation.

Overarching the Deliver stage and all other stages is the primary goal of restorative practice—to repair psychological and emotional damage, to build relationships, and to foster trust between those involved including victim, perpetrator, the school and outer communities. Additionally, it's important to remember that in this stage some disillusionment with restorative practice can arise if you are not seeing results exactly as you envisoned. However, what's important is that progress is made even if it doesn't look perfect right away.

6. Debrief

This is the reflection stage where students look at the ways they succeeded, and ways they could improve their approach in similar future situations.

SF Questions: What were the results of our efforts? How did we succeed or fall short of accomplishing our goal? What went well, and what didn't? How can we improve our efforts and outcome in the future? How can we apply what we've done to similar problems?

RP Questions: What have you learned? How has it changed your relationship with each other/the school/ the community? What will you do differently next time?

The importance of debriefing the process of applying restorative practices to conflict resolution can't be overstated. It's absolutely crucial that all participants engage in follow-up conversations to share progress and to determine next steps.

Questions that can be asked at this stage are:

- How do the involved parties feel about their RP session overall?
- Has everyone completed their responsibilities?
- What have they discovered about themselves and each other?

- What's the one thing above all others each person would like to work to improve?
- What was most difficult about this process?
- What was most rewarding about this process?
- What most got in the way of progress, if anything?
- Have their relationships improved? How have they improved?
- How do they think their behavioural changes have contributed to the school environment?
- How can they apply what they've learned to future situations?
- How can they model the benefits of this experience for their peers?
- Do they have any questions about anything that has happened?

Summary

Now that we've seen how Solution Fluency is used for the facilitation of restorative practices, we can take a brief look in the next chapter at how to manage and audit restorative practices. The guidelines in this chapter will provide a good baseline for you to use as you monitor your school's and district's progress with RP. You'll also be provided with a series of sample worksheets for easier facilitation.

Guiding Questions

- What usually happens after an event or incident that requires conflict resolution?
- Why is it inadvisable to dive right into a restorative practice approach immediately following a confrontation?
- Why is agreement or consent necessary to obtain as a part of restorative practice?
- Why is it crucial for all accounts and viewpoints of an icident to be heard?
- What is the purpose of having both parties in an incident (victim and aggressor) to be involved in working on a solution to their conflict?
- What does the concept of the "unique brain" have to do with restorative practice, especially in regard to young children?

Managing
Restorative Practice

As with any new system that is part of your school culture, RP must be managed and improved by collecting and refining data on how it is being used. Regularly analyzing your collected data is key to determining what is working well and what needs to be improved. It's a big job, however, and it will be ongoing for as long as you choose to work with RP in your school.

The primary challenge presented by proper data collection and analysis is that it takes time. As such, concerns that it takes away from the interactions that are important to successful RP can arise (e.g., time with students, parents, etc.). You'll need to develop a system of accountability that sacrifices neither accurate data collection or building meaningful relationships through RP.

This following charts of questions are based on the analytical framework used by the Denver School-Based Restorative Practices Partnership. It provides an excellent snapshot of the types of RP data that should be analyzed and collected and the purpose it serves. As you go through each section, think about how you could use these questions to audit restorative practices in your own school, and how you would go about using the data you collect for making any adjustments or ammendments to your system for the benefit of both staff and students.

You'll also find some useful worksheets at the back of this resource that will help you with facilitating your Solution Fluency restorative practice gathering. There are sheets included for both participants and facilitators.

1 Survey educators on school climate at regular intervals (at least twice per year)

PURPOSE

- To determine if school climate has improved for educators and how
- To identify areas for additional support or training
- To identify how educators are consistently using restorative practices
- To understand what might be contributing to any existing turnover and/or retention

QUESTIONS

- How has climate improved across the school for this period?
- Where do you think more support and training is necessary?
- How do you feel the staff/students are responding to restorative practices in your school?
- What have been your own experiences with RP?
- What are the benefits/drawbacks?

2 Survey families on school climate at regular intervals (at least twice per year)

PURPOSE

- To determine if school climate has improved for families and how
- To identify areas where more support, communication, or training is needed
- To understand what can improve family engagement
- To understand ways to improve student/family retention

QUESTIONS

- How has school climate improved for families for this period?
- Where do you think more support and training is necessary?
- How can communication/facilitation of RP with parents be improved?
- What other beneficial ways can parents become involved in the restorative practices process?
- What are parent's primary concerns?

3 Survey students on school climate at regular intervals (at least twice per year)

PURPOSE

- To determine if and in what ways school climate has improved for students
- To identify areas in which more support or training is necessary
- To understand ways to improve student engagement
- To understand ways to improve student retention

QUESTIONS

- How has school climate improved for students for this period?
- Where do you think more support and training is necessary?
- How are students responding to RP in your opinion?
- What evidence do you see with student interactions that RP is working/not working?

4 Total percentage of students being referred to the restorative process (at least once per year)

PURPOSE

- To determine what percentage of students are given additional supports in developing conflict resolution and social-emotional skills in order to determine where additional proactive skill building might be needed

QUESTIONS

- How many students have been referred to RP sessions during this period?
- What types of incidents are being reported?
- What trends are you seeing in the data regarding the severity of incidents, how effectively they are resolved, and how long the changes are lasting?
- How are students being supported and counselled post session?

5 Total percentage of educators participating in restorative practices (at least once per year)

PURPOSE

- To determine what percentage of educators are providing and provided with additional support in developing conflict resolution and social-emotional skills in order to determine where additional proactive skill building might be needed

QUESTIONS

- How are teachers being supported in the RP process in your school?
- What is being done to provide them with support?
- How are they supporting others?
- What is their view of how RP is working in your school?
- What do they feel could be improved upon to make their support system better?

6 Behaviour for which students and educators are referred to restorative practices

PURPOSE

- To ensure the behaviours being referred to the RP Coordinator are not behaviours that could be resolved within the classroom
- To identify proactive measures that can be taken to reduce the number of referrals to the restorative process

QUESTIONS

- How many incidents have been recommended for RP this period?
- What has been their primary nature?
- How does the number of referrals compare to previous period reports?
- Are punitive measures being used in your school? If so, to what effect?
- What can be done to reduce the number of referrals for next period?

7 Source of referral to restorative practice (self, educator, parent, peer) for students and educators

PURPOSE

- To measure student and educator understanding of the purpose of restorative practices in order to inform future trainings for students and staff
- Self and peer referrals can be a strong indicator of successful understanding of the vision

QUESTIONS

- How many teachers have made referrals for restorative practices this period?
- How many teachers/students have been referred, and for what reasons?
- Who have been your primary sources of referral?
- In your opinion, what do these referrals indicate regarding the effectiveness of RP in your school?

8 Feedback survey for those who participate in restorative process (per session/period)

PURPOSE

- To determine if participants are satisfied with the results of the restorative process
- To inform adjustments to be made to the restorative process

QUESTIONS

- What do you want to find out about RP in your school and why?
- What are the views of your RP coordinator regarding the effectiveness of RP?
- How will you use the data collected to make adjustments and improvements?
- How will you decide whether to continue using RP in your school?

Restorative Practice Scenarios

The following practice scenarios can be used by staff and students to determine how you will approach incidents in your school environment that call for restorative practice interventions, and also to streamline and revise your current processes. Use the incident reports and facilitator's worksheets we include in this book with these scenarios to get a feel for applying the Solution Fluency framework to restorative practice initiatives.

1. A new Year 6 student is being bullied and harassed by a Year 8 student. The older boy taunts and threatens him regularly, to the point where the younger student is afraid to walk home by himself. He has had difficulty making friends because of the bullying, and he claims the older boy has even leveled physical abuse against him, such as shoving him against the lockers and tripping him in the hallway. His mother has contacted the principal who has suggested hosting a restorative practice meeting as a possible solution.

2. A student has been caught defacing school property. This same student has also missed multiple days at school over the past month, and no explanation has been given for the absences. Attempts to contact the student's parents have been unsuccessful.

3. Two Year 7 students have been brought into the office from their PE class for fighting during a basketball game. The two students have been separated and asked to write a statement about their view of the incident. The PE teacher has heard rumours of the two fighting before and has confronted them about it, and they have both denied the rumours. A restorative conversation has been suggested to get to the root of the problem.

4. A student making their way down a classroom aisle was tripped by another student. There are allegedly two witnesses who saw it happen, but the teacher did not.

5. A young student claims that a group of their classmates was standing in a circle looking at pictures on a phone. They overheard one of them laugh and say, "send them to me." Allegedly the rest of the group agreed, and others began asking for them to be sent to everyone. According to the student, the pictures were partly

undressed selfies of one of the girls in their year. They also claim that they heard someone else in the group bragging about having posted the images of the female student online for a joke.

6. Two Year 8 students have been involved in a bullying incident, and the victim—another Year 8 student—has come forward to school authorities. The incident allegedly took place during the lunch hour off school grounds. It was also witnessed by a local business owner who has come forward to the school administration. According to him, he was initially responding to customer complaints of a disruption happening out front of his business. He claims that when he approached the boys and attempted to break up the confrontation, he was verbally abused and threatened by the two student bullies.

7. Two students were working on a paired assignment, and the teacher had noticed one of them not doing very much of the work. They decided to discuss this with the pair at which point one of the students claimed they had done all the work because the other refused to. At this accusation, the other spoke up and said that her partner had been uncommunicative and uncooperative, and had even claimed at one point that she was better off doing everything herself.

8. A mixed group of boys and girls from various junior grades have allegedly been hurling insults at a group of students of Aboriginal ancestry. The insults have been mostly racial slurs, and lately, the abuse has spread to the formation of an online group rallying against the Aboriginal students' presence in the school. The group suffering the injury have been unable to lead healthy lives at school, and feel threatened every day.

9. A student claims that one of the people in their school Facebook group has posted pictures of them and made some funny comments. They didn't give permission to have the image in question posted, and now others are adding replies and likes. The comments are humorous but are still entirely personal and hurtful. The student wants this to stop, but they are scared that they might lose friends or open themselves up to even worse ridicule and abuse.

10. A teacher claims that one of their students has recently been disruptive in class, and has been spoken to a few times about their behaviour. The student appears

to be a loner and doesn't spend time with anyone during lunch hours or study halls. Before this, the student was always reticent and reserved. According to the teacher, this student threatened another during a class. When the teacher spoke up and tried to restore order, the student in question picked up a chair and hurled it at them. The teacher immediately notified school security for fear of one of her other students being harmed.

RP Solution Fluency Exploration: Define

Name: _____   Date: __ / __ / __

DEFINE

To solve a problem, we have to clearly define what the problem is first. We must decide what needs to be addressed and give proper context to the problem.

What happened?

_____

_____

_____

_____

_____

Who was involved?

_____

_____

_____

Where did the incident take place?

_____

_____

What were the events leading to the conflict?

_____

_____

_____

_____

_____

Notes:

_____

_____

_____

_____

_____

_____

RP Solution Fluency Exploration: Discover

Name: _____   Date: __ / __ / __

This is the stage of researching and gathering and analyzing explicit knowledge about the problem. This helps us to give the problem context so that we can identify with it more easily.

What were you thinking and feeling when the incident took place?

_____

_____

_____

_____

_____

What is the history between the people involved, if any?

_____

_____

_____

_____

_____

What has happened since the incident took place?

_____

_____

_____

_____

_____

Notes:

_____

_____

_____

_____

_____

_____

_____

RP Solution Fluency Exploration: Dream

Name: _____   Date: __ / __ / __

DREAM

Here, we open up the heart and mind to possibilities and visions of a solution the way we wish to see it. This phase is all about imagination, extrapolation, and visualization.

What have you thought most about since this incident?

_____
_____
_____
_____
_____

In terms of repairing the damage done, what do you want to have happen as an outcome from here?

_____
_____
_____
_____
_____

Why do you feel this is the best solution for everyone involved?

_____
_____
_____
_____
_____

Notes:

_____
_____
_____
_____
_____

 Wabisabi

RP Solution Fluency Exploration: Design

Name: _____   Date: __ / __ / __

DESIGN

This is the workshopping phase. Here, the mechanics of your solution take shape. It involves allowing us to work together to help our solution become reality.

What do you think you need to do to make things right?

_____
_____
_____
_____
_____

What are the steps you need to take?

_____
_____
_____
_____
_____

How can we work together to facilitate them?

_____
_____
_____
_____
_____

Notes:

_____
_____
_____
_____
_____
_____

RP Solution Fluency Exploration: Deliver

Name: _____   **Date:** __ / __ / __

DELIVER — In this phase, there are two separate stages—Produce and Publish. This involves the action for completing the product (Produce) and presenting the proposed solution (Publish).

How do we proceed with our solution?

_____
_____
_____
_____
_____

How do we keep track of progress?

_____
_____
_____
_____
_____

How could we address any challenges we have along the way?

_____
_____
_____
_____
_____

Notes:

_____
_____
_____
_____
_____

RP Solution Fluency Exploration: Debrief

Name: _____   Date: __ / __ / __

DEBRIEF *This is the reflection stage where students get to own their learning. They look at the ways they succeeded, and ways they could improve their approach in similar future situations.*

What have you learned looking back on this experience?

_____
_____
_____
_____
_____

How has your relationship changed with each other? How about with your school and your community?

_____
_____
_____
_____
_____

What will you do differently next time?

_____
_____
_____
_____
_____

Notes:

_____
_____
_____
_____
_____

RP Solution Fluency Facilitation: Define

Facilitator's Name: _____   Date: __ / __ / __

Participant's Name:_____

What happened?
_____
_____
_____
_____
_____
_____

Who was involved?
_____
_____
_____

Where did the incident take place?
_____
_____
_____

What were the events leading to the conflict?
_____
_____
_____
_____
_____

Participant's Name:_____

What happened?
_____
_____
_____
_____
_____
_____

Who was involved?
_____
_____
_____

Where did the incident take place?
_____
_____
_____

What were the events leading to the conflict?
_____
_____
_____
_____
_____

DEFINE summary notes:
_____
_____
_____
_____
_____

RP Solution Fluency Facilitation: Discover

Facilitator's Name: _____   Date: __ / __ / __

Participant's Name:_____

What were they thinking and feeling when the incident took place?

_____

_____

_____

_____

_____

What is the history between those involved, if any?

_____

_____

_____

_____

_____

_____

What has happened since the incident took place?

_____

_____

_____

_____

_____

_____

Participant's Name:_____

What were they thinking and feeling when the incident took place?

_____

_____

_____

_____

_____

What is the history between those involved, if any?

_____

_____

_____

_____

_____

_____

What has happened since the incident took place?

_____

_____

_____

_____

_____

_____

DISCOVER summary notes:

_____

_____

_____

_____

_____

RP Solution Fluency Facilitation: Dream

Facilitator's Name: _____   Date: __ / __ / __

Participant's Name:_____	**Participant's Name:**_____
What have they thought most about since this incident?	*What have they thought most about since this incident?*
_____ _____ _____ _____ _____	_____ _____ _____ _____ _____
In terms of repairing the damage done, what do they want to have happen as an outcome from here?	*In terms of repairing the damage done, what do they want to have happen as an outcome from here?*
_____ _____ _____ _____ _____	_____ _____ _____ _____ _____
Why do they feel this is the best solution for everyone involved?	*Why do they feel this is the best solution for everyone involved?*
_____ _____ _____ _____ _____	_____ _____ _____ _____ _____

DREAM summary notes:

_____
_____
_____
_____
_____

 Wabisabi

RP Solution Fluency Facilitation: Design

Facilitator's Name: _____   **Date:** __ / __ / __

Participant's Name:_____	Participant's Name:_____
What do they think they need to do to make things right?	*What do they think they need to do to make things right?*
_____	_____
_____	_____
_____	_____
_____	_____
_____	_____
What are the steps they want to take?	*What are the steps they want to take?*
_____	_____
_____	_____
_____	_____
_____	_____
_____	_____
How do they feel everyone can work together to best facilitate them?	*How do they feel everyone can work together to best facilitate them?*
_____	_____
_____	_____
_____	_____
_____	_____
_____	_____
_____	_____

DESIGN summary notes:

_____

_____

_____

_____

_____

RP Solution Fluency Facilitation: Deliver

Facilitator's Name: _____   Date: __ / __ / __

Participant's Name:_____	Participant's Name:_____
How do they want to proceed with their solution? _____ _____ _____ _____ _____	*How do they want to proceed with their solution?* _____ _____ _____ _____ _____
How will they keep track of progress? _____ _____ _____ _____ _____	*How will they keep track of progress?* _____ _____ _____ _____ _____
How do they want to address any challenges along the way? _____ _____ _____ _____ _____ _____	*How do they want to address any challenges along the way?* _____ _____ _____ _____ _____ _____

DELIVER summary notes:

_____
_____
_____
_____
_____

 Wabisabi

RP Solution Fluency Facilitation: Debrief

Facilitator's Name: _____ Date: __ / __ / __

Participant's Name:_____

What have they learned looking back on this experience?

_____
_____
_____
_____
_____

How do they feel relationships with each other/school/community have improved?

_____
_____
_____
_____
_____

What will they do differently next time conflict arises?

_____
_____
_____
_____
_____
_____
_____

Participant's Name:_____

What have they learned looking back on this experience?

_____
_____
_____
_____
_____

How do they feel relationships with each other/school/community have improved?

_____
_____
_____
_____
_____

What will they do differently next time conflict arises?

_____
_____
_____
_____
_____
_____
_____

DEBRIEF summary notes:

_____
_____
_____
_____

RP Self Reflection Exercise

Name: _____   Date: __ / __ / __

DEFINE

Briefly describe the incident, where it happened, and who was involved.

_____
_____
_____
_____

DISCOVER

What has happened since the incident and what have you thought about?

_____
_____
_____
_____

DREAM

What do you want to see happen and why is the best outcome?

_____
_____
_____
_____

DESIGN

What must we you to make things right? How could we work together?

_____
_____
_____
_____

DELIVER

How do we proceed with our solution? How will we track our progress?

_____
_____
_____
_____

DEBRIEF

What have you learned? What will you do differently next time?

_____
_____
_____

When in Conflict I ...

Name: _____   Date: __ / __ / __

It's important in conflict resolution to practice prevention first. Tick off each box below that best describes how you react in a conflict situation.

When I am in a conflict situation ...	ALWAYS	SOMETIMES	RARELY	NEVER
I try to calm down before I react.				
I do my best to avoid hurting anyone physically or verbally.				
I avoid getting others involved.				
I try to keep the peace first before things get out of hand.				
I respect and listen to the other people involved in the conflict.				
I remember that all my actions have consequences that can affect everyone.				
I imagine how the other person must feel rather than focusing just on me.				
I avoid using bad language and insults.				
I look for ways to solve the problem rather than win the fight or argument.				
I listen to what the other person has to say.				

References

Catholic Education Office of Melbourne. Student Wellbeing (Research Doc). PDF file. 2007. http://web.spgww.catholic.edu.au/documents/policies/restorativejusticeresearch.pdf

Consedine, Jim. *Restorative Justice: Healing the Effects of Crime*. 1995. Lyttelton, N.Z. Ploughshares Publications.

Daly, Kathleen. The Limits of Restorative Justice. PDF file. 2005. http://www.antoniocasella.eu/restorative/Daly_2005.pdf

RPP Denver. School-Wide Restorative Practices: Step by Step. PDF file. 2017. https://www.skidmore.edu/campusrj/documents/Denver-2017-School-Wide-RP-Implementation-Guide.pdf

Watanabe-Crockett, Lee. Churches, Andrew. *Mindful Assessment: The 6 Essential Fluencies of Innovative Learning*. 2017. Bloomington, IN. Solution Tree Press.

Zehr, Howard. *Changing Lenses: A New Focus for Crime and Justice*. 1990. Harrisonburg, VA. Herald Press.